DISCOVERY EDUCATION | SCIENCE TECHBOOK

California
Unit 1
Plant and Animal Needs

To obtain permission(s) or for inquiries, submit a request to:
Discovery Education, Inc.
4350 Congress Street, Suite 700
Charlotte, NC 28209
800-323-9084
Education_Info@DiscoveryEd.com

ISBN 13: 978-1-68220-529-7

Printed in the United States of America.

1 2 3 4 5 6 7 8 9 10 CJH 23 22 21 20 19   A

© Discovery Education | www.discoveryeducation.com

Acknowledgments

Acknowledgment is given to photographers, artists, and agents for permission to feature their copyrighted material.

Cover and inside cover art: RaquelVizcaino / Shutterstock.com

Table of Contents

Unit 1

Concept 1.1

Concept 1.2

Unit Project

Grade K Resources

DISCOVERY
EDUCATION

Dear Parent/Guardian,

This year, your student will be using Science Techbook™, a comprehensive science program developed by the educators and designers at Discovery Education and written to the California Next Generation Science Standards (NGSS). The California NGSS expect students to act and think like scientists and engineers, to ask questions about the world around them, and to solve real-world problems through the application of critical thinking across the domains of science (Life Science, Earth and Space Science, Physical Science).

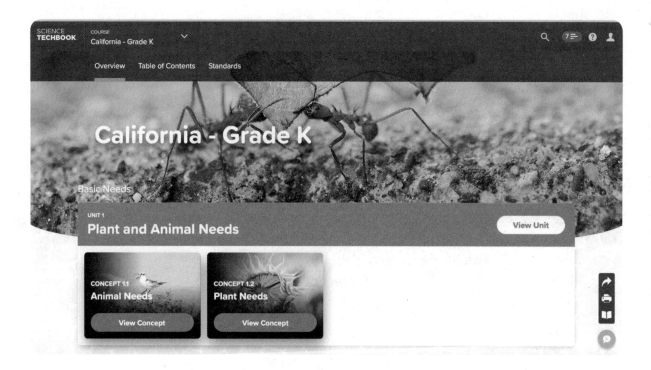

Science Techbook is an innovative program that helps your student master key scientific concepts. Students engage with interactive science materials to analyze and interpret data, think critically, solve problems, and make connections across science disciplines. Science Techbook includes dynamic content, videos, digital tools, Hands-On Activities and labs, and gamelike activities that inspire and motivate scientific learning and curiosity.

You and your child can access the resource by signing in to www.discoveryeducation.com. You can view your child's progress in the course by selecting Assignments.

Science Techbook is divided into units, and each unit is divided into concepts. Each concept has three sections: Wonder, Learn, and Share.

Units and Concepts Students begin to consider the connections across fields of science to understand, analyze, and describe real-world phenomena.

Wonder Students activate their prior knowledge of a concept's essential ideas and begin making connections to a real-world phenomenon and the **Can You Explain?** question.

Learn Students dive deeper into how real-world science phenomenon works through critical reading of the Core Interactive Text. Students also build their learning through Hands-On Activities and interactives focused on the learning goals.

Share Students share their learning with their teacher and classmates using evidence they have gathered and analyzed during Learn. Students connect their learning with STEM careers and problem-solving skills.

Discovery EDUCATION

Within this Student Edition, you'll find QR codes and quick codes that take you and your student to a corresponding section of Science Techbook online. To use the QR codes, you'll need to download a free QR reader. Readers are available for phones, tablets, laptops, desktops, and other devices. Most use the device's camera, but there are some that scan documents that are on your screen.

For resources in California Science Techbook, you'll need to sign in with your student's username and password the first time you access a QR code. After that, you won't need to sign in again, unless you log out or remain inactive for too long.

We encourage you to support your student in using the print and online interactive materials in Science Techbook on any device. Together, may you and your student enjoy a fantastic year of science!

Sincerely,

The Discovery Education Science Team

Unit 1
Plant and Animal Needs

New Puppy

Before getting a new pet, it's important to know what it needs to live and grow. A puppy needs what all living things need. Plants are also living things and have needs. By the end of this unit, you will be able to describe what living things need. You will also be able to match living things to the places where they should live.

New Puppy

Discovery
EDUCATION

Think About It

Look at the pictures. **Think** about the following questions:

- What things do animals need to live and grow?

- What things do plants need to live and grow?

- How does the place where something lives give it what it needs?

Hamster

Investigate Like a Scientist

Quick Code:
ca007s

Hands-On Investigation: Needs of Living Things

In this activity, you will create a habitat. You will choose the living things that can have their needs met in your habitat.

Dry Habitat

SEP	Asking Questions and Defining Problems	CCC	Patterns
SEP	Developing and Using Models	CCC	Cause and Effect
SEP	Analyzing and Interpreting Data	CCC	Systems and System Models

Ask Questions

You are going to create a wet or dry habitat that meets the needs of living things. **Write** some questions you can ask to learn more about it. As you work on activities throughout the unit, **write** down answers to your questions.

Animal Needs

DISCOVERY
EDUCATION

Student Objectives

By the end of this lesson:

☐ I can use evidence to describe how pets meet their needs.

☐ I can use evidence to describe animals that live near me and how they meet their needs.

☐ I can explain how different environments meet the needs of animals.

Key Vocabulary

☐ air
☐ animal
☐ bird
☐ food
☐ grassland

☐ habitat
☐ plant
☐ shelter
☐ survive
☐ water

Quick Code:
ca008s

Activity 1
Can You Explain?

How are animals' needs met by the place in which they live?

_____

_____

_____

_____

_____

_____

_____

Quick Code:
ca010s

Activity 2

Ask Questions Like a Scientist

Quick Code:
ca011s

Needs of Living Things

What do living things need? **Watch** the video. **Think** about the questions.

Let's Investigate Needs of Living Things

Have you ever felt thirsty?

Have you felt hungry?

Have you stayed up late and felt tired?

Have you ever felt too cold or too hot?

What did you need?

Activity 3
Observe Like a Scientist

Quick Code:
ca013s

Pets

Look at the pictures. **Name** the **animals** you see.
Think about what each animal needs.

SEP **Asking Questions and Defining Problems**

CCC **Patterns**

© Discovery Education | www.discoveryeducation.com • Image: Pixabay, Zoom Pet Photography / Getty Images, Pixabay, Mr. Qian / EyeEm / Getty Images

Talk Together

Talk about animals' needs. How are your needs the same as other animals? How are they different?

Activity 4

Evaluate Like a Scientist

Quick Code:
ca016s

What Do You Already Know About Animal Needs?

Discussing Basic Needs

Look at the picture.

Lunchtime

What do you need to **survive**?

Write or **draw** three things you need to survive.

Animals and Places

Match each animal to the place that best meets its needs.

Needs and Wants

What things do you need? What things do you want?

Choose which of these things are needs or wants.

Check the correct box.

Air

☐ Want

☐ Need

Water

☐ Want

☐ Need

Food

☐ Want

☐ Need

Toys

☐ Want

☐ Need

Video Games

☐ Want

☐ Need

Television

☐ Want

☐ Need

What Do Pets Need?

Activity 5

Observe Like a Scientist

Quick Code:
ca020s

The Right Food for Your Pet

 Talk Together

Do you have a pet? Talk to a partner about what you know about taking care of a pet.

SEP Obtaining, Evaluating, and Communicating Information

CCC Patterns

© Discovery Education | www.discoveryeducation.com • Image: Icon: Freepik from www.flaticon.com. Mr. Qian / EyeEm / Getty Images

Watch the video. **Look** for how different pets need different **food**. Then talk together about pet foods.

The Right Food for Your Pet

 Talk Together

Did you notice any patterns? What kind of food do pets need?

Analyze Like a Scientist

Animal Needs

Read about needs. Then **complete** the activity.

Read Together

Animal Needs

Pets are animals. Pets have needs.

Pets

One need is food.

A need is something that must be filled in order to survive.

SEP Obtaining, Evaluating, and Communicating Information

CCC Patterns

Look at the pictures. What other things do animals need?

Circle the things animals need in each picture.

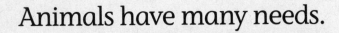

Animals have many needs.

Animals need food. Animals need **water**.
Animals need **shelter**. Animals need **air**
to breathe.

Animals cannot survive without meeting all of
these needs.

Look at the pictures again. **Answer** the questions.
What living thing does the goat need for food?

_____

_____

What living thing does the bear eat?

_____

_____

What non-living thing do the rabbits use for shelter?

_____

_____

Activity 7
Evaluate Like a Scientist

Pets and Food

Match the pets to the food they eat.

Rabbit

Cricket

Lizard

Grass

Bird

Seeds

SEP Obtaining, Evaluating, and Communicating Information

CCC Patterns

What Are the Needs of Animals That Live Around Us?

Activity 8
Observe Like a Scientist

Quick Code:
ca023s

Local Animals

Look at the pictures. How are these animals meeting their needs?

Squirrel

SEP Obtaining, Evaluating, and Communicating Information

CCC Patterns

Discovery EDUCATION

Ants

 Talk Together

What do you see in the pictures that shows that these animals are meeting their needs?

Quick Code:
ca026s

Needs of Local Animals

Read about the needs of local animals. Then, **complete** the activity.

 Read Together

Needs of Local Animals

Animals live all around us.

Local Animals

We can observe them.

We can find out how they meet their needs.

Animals can be large or small.

SEP **Obtaining, Evaluating, and Communicating Information**

Think about an animal that lives outdoors where you live. What are its needs? **Draw** an animal you have observed.

Quick Code:
ca027s

Activity 10

Think Like a Scientist

Animals and Their Needs

In this activity, you will look for different animals. You will determine their needs. Then you will figure out how they meet those needs.

What materials do you need?

- Magnifying glass
- Notebook or paper/clipboard
- Pencils

SEP   **Planning and Carrying Out Investigations**

SEP   **Analyzing and Interpreting Data**

CCC   **Patterns**

© Discovery Education | www.discoveryeducation.com • Image: Mr. Qian / EyeEm / Getty Images

What Will You Do?

Look for animals outside. **Make observations** about the animals and their needs. What did you see?

Think About the Activity

What animals did you observe?

Draw a picture of each animal you observed. **Write** or **draw** what each animal needs. **Show** how it meets its needs.

Animal	Needs of the Animal	Animal Meeting Its Needs

Activity 11

Observe Like a Scientist

Quick Code:
ca028s

Animal Habitats

Watch the video. What is the spider's **habitat**? **Look** for how the spider's habitat helps it meets its needs.

Video

Animal Habitats

 Talk Together

How would you describe the word *habitat*?

SEP **Constructing Explanations and Designing Solutions**

Quick Code:
ca030s

Animal Homes

Read the passage. **Circle** words that describe a habitat.

 Read Together

Animal Homes

Animals live in places that are cold, hot, wet, and dry.

Animals live in habitats.

A habitat provides food, water, and shelter for animals.

Shelter is a home for an animal. Animal homes are not all the same.

A nest would not be a good shelter for a bear.

Bird's Nest

Choose an animal. **Draw** a shelter used by that animal.

SEP Constructing Explanations and Designing Solutions

CCC Patterns

Activity 13

Observe Like a Scientist

Quick Code:
ca031s

Clown Fish

Look at the picture. **Find** things that meet the needs of the fish.

Clown Fish

© Discovery Education | www.discoveryeducation.com • Image: Pixabay, Icon: Freepik from www.flaticon.com, Mr. Qian / EyeEm / Getty Images

Talk Together

Describe the clown fish's habitat. How does this habitat meet the needs of the fish?

SEP Constructing Explanations and Designing Solutions

CCC Cause and Effect

How Do Animals That Live Farther Away Find What They Need to Survive?

 Activity 14
Analyze Like a Scientist

Quick Code:
ca033s

Lions Resting

Look at the picture. Do you think lions and housecats can live in the same habitat? **Read** about the lions. Then **answer** the question.

Lions at Rest

SEP **Engaging in Argument from Evidence**

Lions Resting

Lions are animals. They live on open **grasslands**. They are very fast. They catch other animals to eat.

Lions

All animals need the right kind of place to live. We call this their habitat.

Can lions and housecats live in the same habitat? What words did you read to help you answer the question?

_____

_____

_____

_____

_____

_____

Activity 15
Observe Like a Scientist

Quick Code:
ca035s

Needs of Living Things

Play the Fun-damental. **Think** about the animals that live in each part of the forest.

| SEP | Obtaining, Evaluating, and Communicating Information |
| CCC | Cause and Effect |

© Discovery Education | www.discoveryeducation.com ● Image: Mr. Qian / EyeEm / Getty Images

Write or **draw** animals that live in each part of the forest. Then **write** or **draw** animals that do not live there.

Name of Habitat	Live There	Do Not Live There
Forest floor		
Upper trees		
Fallen log		
Stream		

Activity 16

Evaluate Like a Scientist

Quick Code:
ca036s

Habitat and Needs

Look at the picture. How do the raccoons meet their needs?

Raccoons

SEP   **Engaging in Argument from Evidence**

CCC   **Cause and Effect**

Write or **draw** to show how the raccoons meet their needs.

food	
water	
shelter	

Where Are Living Things Found?

Read about living things. Then, **answer** the question.

 Read Together

Where Are Living Things Found?

Many living things have specific needs.

A **bird** might only eat one type of seed. If a bird cannot find that seed, it will die.

Bird

If living things live in habitats that don't meet their needs, they will not have what they need to live.

Frog

Look at the picture of the frog. Could a frog live in the desert? Why or why not?

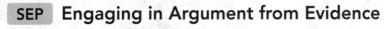

Activity 18
Observe Like a Scientist

Quick Code:
ca038s

Matching Animals and Habitats

Look at the pictures. **Think** about animals' habitats.
Circle any animals that could live in the desert.

Parrot

Sea Lion

Panda

Snake

SEP Constructing Explanations and Designing Solutions

Discovery EDUCATION

Describe each animal's habitat. What are its needs?
Write or **draw** pictures.

Parrot	Sea Lion
Panda	**Snake**

Quick Code:
ca044s

Activity 19
Solve Problems Like a Scientist

Keeping Seals Safe

In this activity, you will build a model of a zoo enclosure where seals will live.

Seal on a Rock

© Discovery Education | www.discoveryeducation.com • Image: Mr. Qian / EyeEm / Getty Images, Hung Ho-EyeEm / EyeEm / Getty Images

SEP   Developing and Using Models

SEP   Constructing Explanations and Designing Solutions

CCC   Systems and System Models

What materials do you need?

- Craft sticks
- Color paper
- Pre-cut cardboard strips
- Tape or glue

The zoo is getting new animals. Seals will be coming soon. Seals eat fish. Seals swim in water. Seals also live on land. The zoo wants to build a new place for them to live. What should this place in the zoo look like?

How will the seals get to water?

How will the seals get up on land?

How will the seals be kept safe from people and other animals?

Where will the seals' food be kept?

Draw a picture of what you think the enclosure will look like.

Explain how your enclosure meets the needs of the seals.

Water	Food
Shelter	**Safety**

Activity 20

Record Evidence Like a Scientist

Quick Code:
ca047s

Needs of Living Things

Now that you have learned about the needs of animals, look again at Needs of Living Things. You first saw this in Wonder.

Video

Let's Investigate Needs of Living Things

 Talk Together

How can you describe Needs of Living Things now? How is your explanation different from before?

SEP   **Constructing Explanations and Designing Solutions**

Look at the Can You Explain? question. You first read this question at the beginning of the lesson.

> **Can You Explain?**
>
> How are animals' needs met by the place in which they live?

How do your new ideas about Needs of Living Things help you answer a question?

1. **Choose** a question. You can use the Can You Explain? question or one of your own. You can also use one of the questions that you wrote at the beginning of the lesson.

   My Question

2. Then **use** the sentence frames on the next page to answer the question.

Animals' needs are

_____

_____

_____

Those needs are met by

_____

_____

_____

My evidence is

_____

_____

_____

I know this because

_____

_____

_____

_____

Discovery
EDUCATION

Activity 21
Analyze Like a Scientist

Helping Animals Meet Their Needs

Read about people who help animals. Then, **try** the activity.

 Read Together

Helping Animals Meet Their Needs

A veterinarian is an animal doctor.

Veterinarians know what animals need.

They help us to keep animals healthy.

SEP Obtaining, Evaluating, and Communicating Information

They know that each animal needs the right kind of food.

They know that animals need water. They also know how to protect animals.

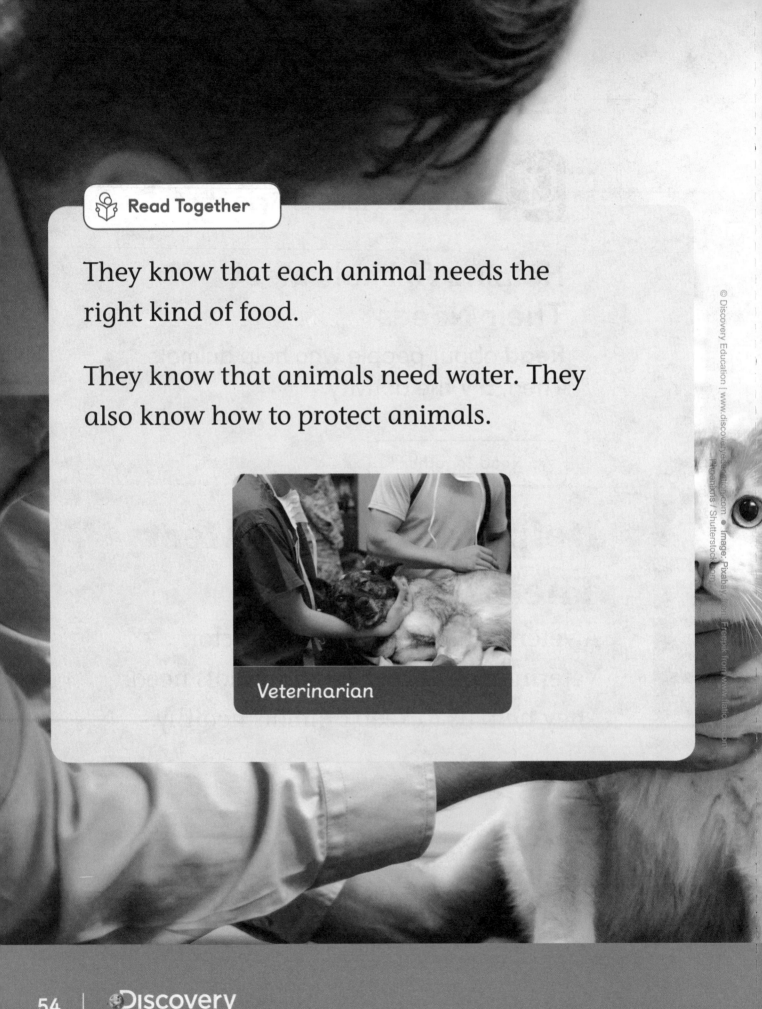

Veterinarian

Park rangers also know a lot about animals. They study wild animals. They know where animals should live. They care for the animals in the park.

This ranger is helping students learn about nature.

Park Ranger

What can a park ranger tell us about the animals in the park?

Veterinarian or Park Ranger?

Veterinarians take care of animals' health. Park rangers take care of the environment in a park. **Draw** lines to match the tools to a veterinarian or a park ranger.

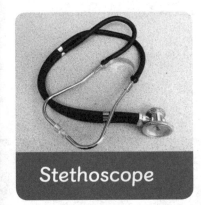

Stethoscope

Binoculars

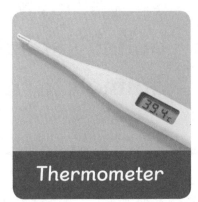

Thermometer

Veterinarian

Park Ranger

Hiking Boots

Hat

Bandages

Discovery
EDUCATION

Activity 22

Evaluate Like a Scientist

Quick Code:
ca051s

Review: Animal Needs

Think about what you have read and seen. What did you learn?

Draw what you have learned. Then **tell** someone else about what you learned.

© Discovery Education | www.discoveryeducation.com ● Image: icon: Freepik from www.flaticon.com, Mr. Qian / EyeEm / Getty Images

 Talk Together

Think about what you saw in Get Started.
Use your new ideas to discuss animals' needs.

CCC **Patterns**

Plant Needs

Student Objectives

By the end of this lesson:

☐ I can look at plants and find patterns in what they need to survive.

☐ I can investigate to find patterns in how plants near me meet their needs.

☐ I can interpret data to find patterns in how plants that live in other places meet their needs.

☐ I can look at a model of a habitat and see how it meets the needs of plants.

Key Vocabulary

☐ basic need   ☐ mineral
☐ grow   ☐ root
☐ light   ☐ soil

Quick Code:
ca057s

Activity 1

Can You Explain?

How are plants' needs met by
the place in which they live?

_____

- -

_____

_____

- -

_____

_____

- -

_____

_____

Quick Code:
ca059s

DISCOVERY EDUCATION

Activity 2
Ask Questions Like a Scientist

Quick Code:
ca062s

Healthy Plants

There is a story behind every picture. **Look** at the pictures of the plants.

Let's Investigate Healthy Plants

| SEP | **Asking Questions and Defining Problems** |

| CCC | **Cause and Effect** |

What happened to the plant in the pot? **Talk** with a partner about your ideas.

We don't know why one plant looks different from the other plant. It is a mystery.

What questions do you have about the mystery?

Activity 3
Investigate Like a Scientist

Quick Code:
ca060s

Hands-On Investigation: What Do Plants Need?

In this activity, you will **see** what a plant needs to survive.

Make a Prediction

What happens if a plant does not meet its needs?

What materials do you need?

- 2 containers for seedlings
- Potting soil
- Open container for soil
- Small measuring spoons
- 6 seeds
- Small envelope
- Eye dropper

- Large, clear plastic bags
- Half-inch tubing, 8 inches
- Rubber stopper
- Scissors
- Tape
- Hand lens

SEP Planning and Carrying Out Investigations

CCC Cause and Effect

What Will You Do?

Watch the video.

What Do Plants Need?

Video

Plant seeds in soil. **Watch** what happens to the seeds.

Draw the plant at four different times. How does it change?

Day ___	Day ___
Day ___	**Day ___**

Test what happens when the plant does not get fresh air. **Write** or **draw** how you will test this.

DISCOVERY
EDUCATION

Draw each plant for seven days.

Day	Fresh Air	No Fresh Air
1		
2		
3		

Day	Fresh Air	No Fresh Air
4		
5		
6		
7		

Discovery
EDUCATION

Activity 4
Analyze Like a Scientist

Quick Code:
ca065s

Thinking About What Plants Need

Read about what plants need. Then **complete** the activity.

> Read Together

Thinking About What Plants Need

Just like animals, plants need some things to live.

The first plant is healthy.

Its needs have been met.

The second plant is not healthy.

Its leaves are drooping.

Draw a picture of a plant that is healthy.

Draw a picture of a plant that is not healthy.

SEP Asking Questions and Defining Problems

CCC Cause and Effect

Activity 5
Evaluate Like a Scientist

Quick Code:
ca066s

What Do You Already Know About Plant Needs?

Taking Care of Plants

Look at the picture carefully.

House Plants

Think about the picture.

Complete the sentences.

Choose the right word.

> light   soil   water

The woman is giving the plants _____.

The plants get _____ through the window.

The plants **grow** in pots. The pots have _____.

Where Does It Belong?

Match each plant with the place where you find it.

Forest

Beach

Pond

Desert

What Do Plants Need to Grow?

Activity 6

Observe Like a Scientist

Quick Code:
ca068s

How Do Plants Grow?

Watch the video. **Look** for the tools used by the student scientists.

How Do Plants Grow?

© Discovery Education | www.discoveryeducation.com ● Image: Pixabay, Junichi Koga / EyeEm / Getty Images

SEP   Obtaining, Evaluating, and Communicating Information

Talk Together

What tools did the students use?

Why did students use those tools to measure the plants?

What Do Plants Need to Grow?

Plants have many needs.

Plants need **light**. Plants use light to make their food.

Roots

Plants need water and **minerals**.

Most plants use their **roots** to get water and minerals from the soil.

Plants need air.

Plants need a temperature that is not too hot or too cold.

Plants cannot survive very long without meeting all of these needs.

What Do Plants Need to Grow?

What do plants need to survive? **Write** or **draw** four things plants need.

What Plants Need	

SEP Obtaining, Evaluating, and Communicating Information

CCC Cause and Effect

Quick Code:
ca071s

Activity 8
Observe Like a Scientist

Getting to Know Plants

Play the Fun-damental. **Complete** the Seed to Shiny Seed section.

SEP   **Developing and Using Models**

CCC   **Cause and Effect**

Draw a picture of a seed in soil. **Label** two things the seed needs to grow.

[drawing box]

Draw a picture of a seedling. **Include** three things the seedling needs to grow into a plant.

[drawing box]

Activity 9
Investigate Like a Scientist

Quick Code:
ca072s

Hands-On Investigation: What Do Plants Need?

In this activity, you will **see** if a plant needs air to survive. You have been collecting data.

Think About the Activity

Draw a picture of a plant meeting its needs.

SEP **Planning and Carrying Out Investigations**

SEP **Analyzing and Interpreting Data**

CCC **Patterns**

  **Discovery** EDUCATION

What was the same about how you cared for each plant? **Draw** or **write** your answer.

[ ]

What was different about how you cared for each plant? **Draw** or **write** your answer.

[ ]

Do plants need air to survive? How do you know?

_____

_____

_____

_____

_____

What did you see with the hand lens? **Draw** or **write** your answer.

| **Discovery** EDUCATION

What Are the Needs of Plants That Live Around Us?

Activity 10

Observe Like a Scientist

Quick Code:
ca073s

How Plants Live and Grow

Watch the video. **Look** for ways plants help people meet their **basic needs**.

How Plants Live and Grow

SEP Engaging in Argument from Evidence

CCC Cause and Effect

Talk Together

What would the world be like if there were not any plants?

What Are the Needs of the Plants That Live Around Us?

Read about plants.

 Read Together

What Are the Needs of the Plants That Live Around Us?

Plants live all around us.

We can observe them.

We can find out how they meet their needs.

SEP Obtaining, Evaluating, and Communicating Information

CCC Patterns

Think about the plants that live outdoors where you live.

Some may be tall, like trees. Some may be short, like grass. Some may live in sunshine. Some may live in shade.

How do they meet their needs?

Forest

DISCOVERY
EDUCATION

Draw a picture of a plant you observed outside.

Activity 12
Observe Like a Scientist

Quick Code:
ca076s

Forest and Moss

Look at the pictures. **Think** about the different needs of the plants.

Forest

Moss

 Talk Together

What are the plants' needs? How are their needs different?

SEP **Constructing Explanations and Designing Solutions**

CCC **Energy and Matter**

Activity 13

Think Like a Scientist

Quick Code:
ca078s

Plant Search

In this activity, you will find and draw plants.

What materials do you need?

- Paper
- Pencil
- Colored pencils or markers

What Will You Do?

Find plants outside.

Look carefully at the plant.

Draw the plants you find.

SEP	Constructing Explanations and Designing Solutions
SEP	Engaging in Argument from Evidence
SEP	Planning and Carrying Out Investigations
CCC	Patterns

Plants in My Environment

Think About It

Look at your drawings.

How many tall plants did you draw?

How many short plants did you draw?

What patterns did you notice?

_____

_____

_____

How do the plants meet their needs?

_____

_____

_____

How Do Plants That Live Farther Away Meet Their Needs?

Activity 14

Observe Like a Scientist

Quick Code:
ca079s

Mangrove Forest

Look at the picture. **Think** about how the mangrove meets its basic needs.

Mangrove Forest

SEP **Obtaining, Evaluating, and Communicating Information**

CCC **Patterns**

Talk Together

How are the basic needs of the mangrove the same as the basic needs of moss?

How are they different?

Quick Code:
ca080s

Plant Habitats

Read about plant habitats. Then **complete** the activity.

🧑‍🏫 Read Together

Plant Habitats

Some plants need to live in a place with a lot of water.

Marsh

Other plants can live in dry places. All plants need the right kind of place to live.

We call this their habitat.

| SEP | Obtaining, Evaluating, and Communicating Information |
| CCC | Patterns |

Think about the habitats you observed this school year. **Draw** a picture of a plant in a habitat you observed.

Activity 16

Think Like a Scientist

Why Does It Live in That Habitat?

In this activity, you will look at plants that live in other places.

What materials do you need?

- Photos of plants
- Brown crayon
- Blue crayon
- Yellow crayon
- Red crayon

What Will You Do?

Look at the pictures of plants.

SEP Constructing Explanations and Designing Solutions

CCC Patterns

Color the sunlight yellow.

Circle water in blue.

Circle soil in brown.

Write C in red on a place that is cold.

Write H in red on a place that is hot.

Write M in red on a place that is mild.

Talk Together

Where did the plants get light?

Where did the plants get water?

Where did the plants grow?

How did the plants get what they needed to live?

Activity 17

Record Evidence Like a Scientist

Quick Code:
ca092s

Healthy Plants

Now that you have learned about the needs of plants, look again at Healthy Plants. You first saw this in Wonder.

Let's Investigate Healthy Plants

Talk Together

How can you describe the Healthy Plant mystery now? How is your explanation different from before?

SEP Constructing Explanations and Designing Solutions

Look at the Can You Explain? question. You first read this question at the beginning of the lesson.

 Can You Explain?

How are plants' needs met by the place in which they live?

How do your new ideas about Healthy Plants help you answer a question?

1. **Choose** a question. You can use the Can You Explain? question or one of your own. You can also use one of the questions that you wrote at the beginning of the lesson.

My Question

2. Then **use** the sentence frames on the next page to answer the question.

Write a scientific explanation to answer the question.

Use the sentence frames to help you.

Plant needs are

_____

_____

_____

Those needs are met by

_____

_____

_____

Discovery
EDUCATION

My evidence is

I know this because

Activity 18

Analyze Like a Scientist

Quick Code:
ca095s

Working to Meet Plants' Needs

Read about meeting plants' needs.

 Read Together

Working to Meet Plants' Needs

Garden Flowers

Gardeners know about basic needs.

They understand the basic needs of plants.

They know plants need soil.

They know plants need sunlight and water.

They need to make smart decisions to help their garden grow.

Some gardens have plants that you can eat. Some gardens look pretty.

Some gardens do both!

Some gardens grow inside special buildings.

These buildings are called greenhouses.

Greenhouses help keep plants safe and warm.

Greenhouse

Planting a Garden

A gardener wants to plant a new vegetable garden. He wants to put it in a place where his plants will have all their needs met. Where should he place his garden? **Circle** the habitat that meets the plants' needs.

Activity 19

Evaluate Like a Scientist

Quick Code:
ca099s

Review: Plant Needs

Think about what you have read and seen. What did you learn?

Draw what you have learned. Then **tell** someone else about what you learned.

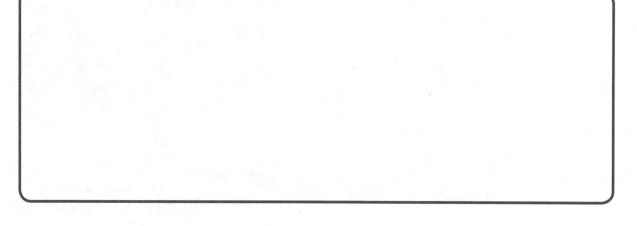

 Talk Together

Think about what you saw in Get Started. Use your new ideas to discuss plants' needs.

CCC Patterns

Investigate Like a Scientist

Quick Code:
ca103s

Hands-On Investigation: Needs of Living Things

In this activity, you will make a wet or dry habitat.

Dry Habitat

SEP	Asking Questions and Defining Problems	CCC	Patterns
SEP	Developing and Using Models	CCC	Cause and Effect
SEP	Analyzing and Interpreting Data	CCC	Systems and System Models

What materials do you need?

- Small box or container

- Soil

- Sand

- Water

- Plant food

- Grass

- Cactus

- Flowers

- Algae or seaweed

- Grasshopper

- Sand crab

- Goldfish

- More sunlight

- Less sunlight

- Heavy rain

- Less rain

Unit Project

Ask Questions

How will you create a wet or dry habitat? What living things will live in your habitat?

What nonliving things will be part of your habitat?

Draw a picture of your habitat design.

What Will You Do?

Make your habitat.

Test your design.

Draw or **write** to show how you tested it.

Think About the Activity

Write or **draw** your answers to the questions in the chart.

How well did your design meet the needs of living things? How could you make your design better?

What Worked?	What Didn't Work?

What Could Work Better?

Grade K Resources

- Bubble Map
- Safety in the Science Classroom
- Vocabulary Flash Cards
- Glossary
- Index

Name _____

Bubble Map

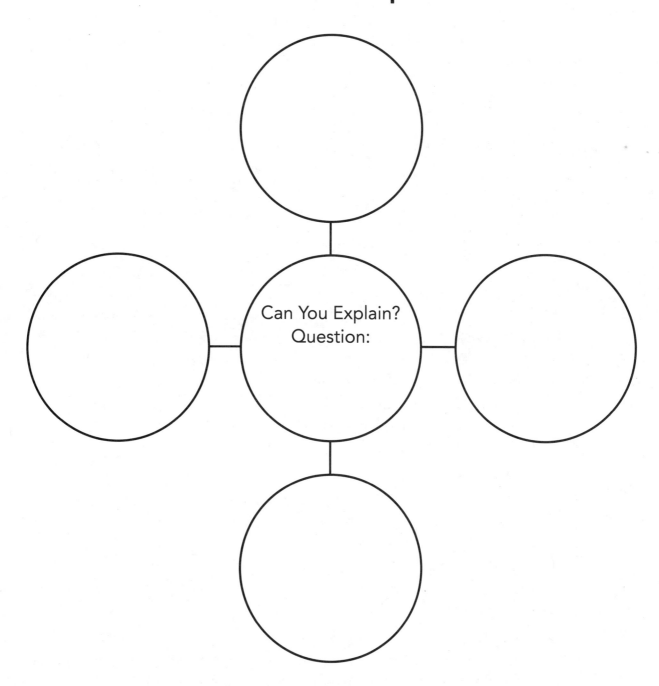

Can You Explain?
Question:

Safety in the Science Classroom

Following common safety practices is the first rule of any laboratory or field scientific investigation.

Dress for Safety

One of the most important steps in a safe investigation is dressing appropriately.

- Splash goggles need to be kept on during the entire investigation.

- Use gloves to protect your hands when handling chemicals or organisms.

- Tie back long hair to prevent it from coming in contact with chemicals or a heat source.

Safety Goggles

- Wear proper clothing and clothing protection. Roll up long sleeves, and if they are available, wear a lab coat or apron over your clothes. Always wear closed-toe shoes. During field investigations, wear long pants and long sleeves.

Be Prepared for Accidents

Even if you are practicing safe behavior during an investigation, accidents can happen. Learn the emergency equipment location in your classroom and how to use it.

- The eye and face wash station can help if a harmful substance or foreign object gets into your eyes or onto your face.

- Fire blankets and fire extinguishers can be used to smother and put out fires in the laboratory. Talk to your teacher about fire safety in the lab. He or she may not want you to directly handle the fire blanket and fire extinguisher. However, you should still know where these items are in case the teacher asks you to retrieve them.

Most importantly, when an accident occurs, immediately alert your teacher and classmates. Do not try to keep the accident a secret or respond to it by yourself. Your teacher and classmates can help you.

Fire Extinguisher

Practice Safe Behavior

There are many ways to stay safe during a scientific investigation. You should always use safe and appropriate behavior before, during, and after your investigation.

- Read all of the steps of the procedure before beginning your investigation. Make sure you understand all the steps. Ask your teacher for help if you do not understand any part of the procedure.

- Gather all your materials and keep your workstation neat and organized. Label any chemicals you are using.

- During the investigation, be sure to follow the steps of the procedure exactly. Use only directions and materials that have been approved by your teacher.

Discovery
EDUCATION

- Eating and drinking are not allowed during an investigation. If asked to observe the odor of a substance, do so using the correct procedure known as wafting, in which you cup your hand over the container holding the substance and gently wave enough air toward your face to make sense of the smell.

- When performing investigations, stay focused on the steps of the procedure and your behavior during the investigation. During investigations, there are many materials and equipment that can cause injuries.

- Treat animals and plants with respect during an investigation.

- After the investigation is over, appropriately dispose of any chemicals or other materials that you have used. Ask your teacher if you are unsure of how to dispose of anything.

- Make sure that you have returned any extra materials and pieces of equipment to the correct storage space.

- Leave your workstation clean and neat. Wash your hands thoroughly.

air

Image: Discovery Communications, Inc.

an invisible gas that is all around us; living things need it to breathe and grow

animal

Image: Discovery Communications, Inc.

a living thing that moves around to look for food, water, or shelter, but can't make its own food

basic need

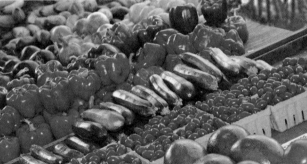
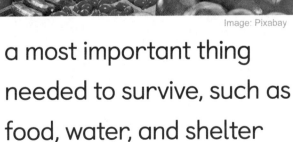

Image: Pixabay

a most important thing needed to survive, such as food, water, and shelter

bird

Image: Discovery Communications, Inc.

an animal with feathers, wings, and a beak whose babies are born from eggs

food

Image: YinYang / E+ / Getty Images

what living things need to eat so they can grow and survive

grassland

Image: Paul Fuqua

a large area of land covered by grass

grow

Image: Pixabay

to get larger

habitat

Image: Paul Fuqua

the place where a plant or animal lives

light

Image: Discovery Education

a form of energy that makes it possible for your eyes to see

mineral

Image: IvanDonHuan/Shutterstock

something that is formed in the earth and is not part of a plant or animal

plant

Image: Paul Fuqua

a living thing made up of cells that needs water and sunlight to survive

root

Image: Paul Fuqua

the part of a plant that usually grows under the ground

shelter

Image: Discovery Education

a place that protects you from harm or bad weather

soil

Image: bluedog studio/Shutterstock

dirt that covers Earth, in which plants can grow and insects can live

survive

Image: Monkey Business Images / Shutterstock.com

to continue to live

water

Image: Paul Fuqua

a clear liquid that has no taste or smell

English —————— **A** —————— **Español**

air

an invisible gas that is all around us; living things, such as plants and animals, need it to breathe and grow

aire

gas invisible que nos rodea; todos los seres vivos, como las plantas y los animales, lo necesitan para respirar y crecer

animal

a living thing that moves around to look for food, water, or shelter, but can't make its own food

animal

ser vivo que se mueve para buscar alimento, agua o refugio, pero no puede producir su propio alimento

—————— **B** ——————

balanced

when something has equal weight or force on both sides

equilibrado

cuando algo tiene un peso o fuerza igual en ambos lados

basic need

a most important thing needed to survive, such as food, water, and shelter

necesidad básica

lo más importante que se necesita para sobrevivir, como alimento, agua y refugio

bird

an animal with feathers, wings, and a beak whose babies are born from eggs

ave

animal que tiene plumas, alas y un pico cuyos bebés nacen de huevos

blizzard

a very big snowstorm

ventisca

tormenta de nieve muy grande

— C —

chemical

created when certain substances are mixed together

sustancia química

se forma cuando se mezclan otras sustancias

cloud

a group of water droplets
or ice crystals that form
together in the sky

nube

grupo de gotitas de agua
o cristales de hielo que
se forman en el cielo

compare

to look at two or more
things to see what is the
same and different

comparar

observar dos o más
cosas para ver en qué se
parecen y se diferencian

———————— D ————————

data

information that is
used to learn about
something

dato

información que se usa
para aprender acerca
de algo

describe

to tell or write about
something, like creating
a picture with words

describir

contar o escribir acerca
de algo, como crear un
dibujo con palabras

design

a plan of how to create
or build something

diseño

plan de cómo crear o
construir algo

direction

the line in which a person
or object is moving

dirección

línea en la que se mueve
una persona u objeto

——————— E ———————

energy

the ability to do work or
make something change

energía

habilidad de trabajar o
producir un cambio

engineer

a person who designs
something that may
be helpful to solve a
problem

ingeniero

persona que diseña algo
que puede ser útil para
resolver un problema

environment

all the living and nonliving things that surround an organism

medio ambiente

todos los seres vivos y objetos sin vida que rodean a un organismo

---

F

---

food

what living things need to eat so they can grow and survive

alimento

lo que los seres vivos necesitan comer para crecer y sobrevivir

---

force

a push or a pull on an object

fuerza

acción de atraer o empujar que se aplica a un objeto

---

forecast

a prediction of what the weather will be like

pronóstico

predicción sobre cómo será el tiempo

friction

a force that happens when two objects rub together

fricción

fuerza que ocurre cuando se frota un objeto con otro

function

purpose

función

propósito

—— G ——

gas

a liquid made from crude oil and used as a fuel for objects, such as cars

gasolina

líquido hecho a partir del petróleo que se usa como combustible en algunos objetos, como los carros

grassland

a large area of land covered by grass

pradera

gran área de tierra cubierta de hierba

Discovery EDUCATION

gravity

the force that pulls an object toward the center of Earth

gravedad

fuerza que tira de un objeto hacia el centro de la Tierra

grow

to get larger

crecer

hacerse más grande

— H —

habitat

the place where a plant or animal lives

hábitat

lugar donde vive una planta o un animal

hurricane

a big storm with strong winds and a lot of rain

huracán

gran tormenta con vientos fuertes y mucha lluvia

I

information

facts or knowledge that come from a source, such as a book or a person

información

datos o conocimientos que provienen de una fuente, como un libro o una persona

L

landscape

the view of a land's surface

paisaje

vista de la superficie de un terreno

light

a form of energy that makes it possible for our eyes to see

luz

forma de energía que hace posible ver con los ojos

living

things that are alive, such as people and animals

vivo

seres que viven, como las personas y los animales

M

material

things that can be used to build or create something

material

cosas que se pueden usar para construir o crear algo

measure

to find the amount, the weight, or the size of something

medir

hallar la cantidad, el peso o el tamaño de algo

measurement

information that tells us about the amount, the weight, or the size of something

medida

información que nos dice sobre la cantidad, el peso o el tamaño de algo

metal

a shiny material that can be used to make tools and machines

metal

material brillante que se puede usar para hacer herramientas y máquinas

meteorologist

a person who studies weather

meteorólogo

persona que estudia el tiempo

mineral

something that is formed in the earth and is not part of a plant or animal

mineral

algo que se forma en la tierra y no es parte de una planta o animal

model

a human-made version created to show the parts of something else, either big or small

modelo

versión creada por el hombre para mostrar las partes de algo más, ya sea grande o pequeño

motion

going from one place to another

movimiento

ir de un lugar a otro

Discovery
EDUCATION

N

natural resource

a material that comes from Earth and is found in nature

recurso natural

material que proviene de la Tierra y se encuentra en la naturaleza

nonliving

things that are not alive, such as a ball or block

sin vida

cosas que no están vivas, como una pelota o un bloque

O

observe

to watch closely

observar

mirar atentamente

organism

a living thing

organismo

ser vivo

P

plant

a living thing made up of cells that needs water and sunlight to survive

planta

ser vivo formado por células que necesita agua y luz solar para sobrevivir

pollution

when garbage, smells, or other materials are scattered over places that used to be clean

contaminación

cuando la basura, el olor u otros materiales se dispersan en lugares que solían ser limpios

predict

to make a guess based on what you already know

predecir

adivinar en base a lo que ya se sabe

R

record

to write down or make note of something

registrar

escribir o anotar algo

recycle

to create new materials from something used

reciclar

crear nuevos materiales a partir de algo usado

reduce

to use less of something

reducir

usar menos de algo

renewable

to make new again

renovable

hacer que algo sea nuevo otra vez

reuse

to use something again

reutilizar

usar algo de nuevo

root

the part of a plant that usually grows under the ground

raíz

parte de una planta que por lo general crece bajo tierra

S

season

a time of year: summer, autumn, winter, or spring

estación

época del año: el verano, el otoño, el invierno o la primavera

shelter

a place that protects you from harm or bad weather

refugio

lugar para protegerse de peligros o el mal tiempo

soil

dirt that covers Earth, in which plants can grow and insects can live

suelo

tierra que cubre nuestro planeta en la que pueden crecer plantas y vivir insectos

study

a close look at something

estudio

vistazo detallado de algo

sun

any star around which planets revolve

sol

toda estrella alrededor de la cual giran los planetas

survive

to continue to live

sobrevivir

continuar viviendo

— T —

temperature

the measure of how hot or cold something is

temperatura

medida de lo caliente o frío algo está

thermometer

a tool used to measure temperature

termómetro

instrumento que se usa para medir la temperatura

tornado

a storm that creates
a funnel cloud with
extremely fast winds

tornado

tormenta que crea
una nube con forma
de embudo que tiene
vientos extremadamente
rápidos

—————— V ——————

vegetable

a plant or part of a plant
that is used for food

vegetal

planta o parte de una
planta que se usa
como alimento

—————— W ——————

warm

having heat

cálido

que tiene calor

waste

garbage or other
materials you don't need

deshecho

basura u otros materiales
que no necesitamos

Discovery EDUCATION

water

a clear liquid that has no taste or smell

agua

líquido transparente que no tiene sabor ni olor

---

weather

the state of the outdoors at a given time and place

tiempo atmosférico

el estado del exterior en un momento y lugar dados

---

wildlife

plants and animals that live in nature

vida silvestre

plantas y animales que viven en la naturaleza

Index

A

Air
- animals and 22
- mangrove 16
- plants and 60, 64–69, 78, 79, 82–84, 102–105

Analyze Like a Scientist 20–22, 26–27, 32–33, 35–37, 42–43, 53–56, 71–72, 79, 87–89, 96–97, 106–108

Animal habitats
- clown fish 34
- creating 4–5
- defined 32–33, 36
- in different parts of forest 38–39
- frog 42–43
- lion 35–37
- matching animals with 44–45
- raccoon 40–41
- seal 46–49
- spider 31

Animal needs
- air 16, 22
- basic 14–17
- in different parts of forest 38–39
- helping animals meet 53–56
- investigating 10–11
- of local animals 26–27
- place in which they live and 8
- predicting for animals found 28–30
- of raccoons 40–41
- specific 42–43